# 1000 SAYINGS BY OLD FOLKS WHO RAISED US

## WM ROCKY BROWN, 3RD

Quantum
Discovery
A LITERARY AGENCY

*Library of Congress Control Number: 2024927625*

ISBN
979-8-89641-034-8 (Paperback)
979-8-89641-035-5 (eBook)
979-8-89641-057-7 (Hardcover)

# "1000 Sayings by Old Folks Who Raised Us"

Wm Rocky Brown, 3rd

# PREFACE

Let me begin by saying that God is the Head of my life, Jesus is my Savior and the Holy Spirit is my Comforter.

Our parents or grandparents, who had roots in the South, raised many of us. Now, along with that Southern raising came the ability to take every day activities or things of nature and turn them into wise sayings. My mother was from Greenville, North Carolina and my grandmother who raised me was from Mobile, Alabama. They both had old sayings from 'Down Home' that took me a while to really understand what they were saying. After talking to others, I realized that I wasn't the only one who had this wonderful experience growing up, so I decided to compile these 1000 sayings.

It's is my hope that they will bring you fond memories and laughter and you will share them with your children and grandchildren.

This book is dedicated to my mother Gwendolyn Regina Carraway Brown and my grandmothers:

Ethel-Mae Knight Brown (Mother-dear), Halease Moore Wooten-Reid and my great-grandmothers Willie-Mae Knight and Carrie Skipper. My grands are the women on the cover and that's me at 2 months old. (By the way, that's a design on the chair and not a ribbon in my hair. lol)

Special thanks to my friend Ellen Graham, my Bethany Baptist Church members, my Facebook friends and the contributions I found that were posted on the internet by others who also enjoy these sayings.

Enjoy my friends!

WRB, 3rd

# "1000 SAYINGS BY OLD FOLKS WHO RAISED US"

Compiled by Wm. Rocky Brown, 3rd

1. I'm fixin' to

2. You reap what you sow

3. You can lead a horse to the water, but you can't make him drink. But you can salt his oats

4. Going down yonder

5. Sit down and behave

6. Ain't got enough sense to pour piss out of a boot with instructions on the bottom

7. Wrench me that...

8. What is hidden in the dark comes out in the light

9. One for the money Two for the show Three to get ready and Four to go

10. The pot talking about the kettle

11.   The top calling the pot black

12.   You ain't nothing until you're something

13.   I used to walk to school uphill both ways in the winter with no shoes

14.   Get up lazy bones

15.   I got eyes in the back of my head

16.   Rat now

17.   Chidlinns'

18.   Don't you suck your teeth or roll your eyes when I'm talking to you

19.   Don't make me smack the piss outta you

20.   Pee on the fire and call in the dogs this hunt is over

21. *Walked right by me and didn't say cat, dog, or nuthin'*

22. *Do me one mo' gin*

23. *I'll knock yo' fool head off*

24. *One thing for sure and two for certain*

25. *I will knock your block off*

26. *You can take it Or leave it*

27. *Bout to have a conniption*

28. *Young-ins*

29. *Dumb as a doorknob*

30. *I bought you into this world and I'll take you out*

31.   Happy as a pig eating slop

32.   Great day in the morning

33.   Wat us gonna do

34.   Colored folks...

35.   Wretch-around here and get my Bible...

36.   Boy pull up ya britches

37.   You ain't no kin uh mine

38.   That's her Lil red wagon she can push it or pull it

39.   I'm ma beat yo ass

40.   Fair to Midlin

41. *I Reckon*

42. *Come on in the room where Jesus is the Doctor and get my oil*

43. *If it was a snake it would of jumped up and bit you*

44. *All righty now*

45. *Too big for your britches*

46. *Come in here & get grandmamma the rollin pin*

47. *A hard head make a soft behind*

48. *Every tub must stand on its own bottom*

49. *Finnina go*

50. *He is Casket Sharp*

51.    *Over yonder*

52.    *Gan gech me a switch na*

53.    *Please be seen and not heard*

54.    *Southerners that moved North always referred to the South as DOWN HOME*

55.    *Wretch this here glass out for me*

56.    *Is pig meat greasy*

57.    *Child that boy is sewing his oats*

58.    *Every shut eye ain't sleep and every goodbye ain't gone*

59.    *Can't see the forest for the trees*

60.    *Get your behind out of the road*

61.  *Bless his heart*

62.  *I declare*

63.  *Lawdie, Lawdie, I reckon you right*

64.  *If it don't come out in the wash, it'll sure come out in the rinse*

65.  *Money don't grow on trees*

66.  *Come on y'all*

67.  *What goes around comes around*

68.  *Don't dish it if you can't take it*

69.  *They were like two peas in a pod*

70.  *Slap the taste out yo mouth*

71. It takes two to tango

72. This is gonna hurt me more than hurt you

73. My stars and garters

74. You look like the wreck of the Hesperus

75. Your ears are so dirty you could grow tatters in there

76. You'd lose your head if it wasn't attached

77. If your friend jumped off a bridge, would you

78. I wouldn't give you two cents for that

79. You made your bed, now lie in it

80. Liar, liar, pants on fire

81.   Starve a cold, feed a fever

82.   Lawd have mercy

83.   A watched pot never boils

84.   Ain't that the truth

85.   Blood is thicker than water

86.   Cat got your tongue

87.   Butter him up

88.   You always hurt the one you love

89.   Easy as falling off a log

90.   Ain't nothing going on but the rent

91. I can't hear my yeers

92. Grab every rag and string

93. The Lord willing and the creek don't rise

94. Y'all don't believe fat meat is greasy

95. First and last time

96. Sooner or later

97. Kids in Africa are starving and you don't want to eat

98. There is a tag for every rag

99. Taint dat da truth

100. Negroes and flies I do despise the more I see negroes the better I like flies

101.   *You have to dot every "I" and cross every "T"*

102.   *Snake bites you once its the snakes fault, snake bites you twice its your fault*

103.   *Just because the car looks good doesn't mean the oil is clean*

104.   *I'll slap you into the middle of next week*

105.   *I'm as full as a tick*

106.   *You don't think your sh*t stink*

107.   *Haven't seen that sense Skippy was a puppy*

108.   *We going to the store and make groceries*

109.   *Go get me a pop*

110.   *Shumoan here right now*

111. *A top for every pot*

112. *Don't have a pot to piss in or a window to throw it out*

113. *Look at me when I'm talking to you*

114. *What's love got to do with it*

115. *Children are to be seen and not heard*

116. *Great Day in the morning*

117. *I'll slap the black off ya*

118. *Birds of a feather, flock together*

119. *Stop running your mouth*

120. *I don't care what other children do, you're my child*

121.   *You are old enough for your wants not to hurt you*

122.   *As long as you are living in my house, don't you ever...*

123.   *As long as you are living in my house, eating my food, sucking up my heat, wearing my clothes...etc. You will follow my rules*

124.   *Negroes in Hell want ice water*

125.   *I can show you better than I can tell you*

126.   *He's in a heap of trouble*

127.   *Now you cooking with fish grease*

128.   *Lies have short legs and they soon run out*

129.   *Quiet as it's kept*

130.   *Don't let the left hand know what right hand is doing*

131.  Tain't wise

132.  Ain't no fool like an old fool

133.  You got sum tee

134.  Rat a way

135.  She is smelling her pee

136.  He is smelling himself

137.  Boy I seen you before you seen yourself

138.  Big Poppa

139.  Big Momma

140.  Mother-dear

141. I'm looking at you with my good eye

142. If the cow can jump over the level, then I can look at the devil

143. Fresh as dish water

144. Ain't the size of the ship that makes you sick, it's the motion in the ocean

145. Watch out there now

146. He ain't got nuff sense to bella a buzzard

147. Lord help me before I kill this child

148. I'm still holding on

149. No matter how high a bird flies he has to come back down to the ground to eat.

150. Get off your rusty dusty and do what I told you to do

151. *You better ask God to put a jet in your behind*

152. *Won't He do it*

153. *Don't you ever*

154. *Been there, done that, got the T-Shirt to prove it*

155. *There's nothing new underneath the sun*

156. *Don't let the door hit you, where the good Lord split you*

157. *You have to crawl before you walk.*

158. *Loose lips sink ships*

159. *Someone has to haul the ashes*

160. *The early bird catches the worm*

161. *When grown folks are talking stay in a child's place*

162. *Sharp as a tack*

163. *Clean as the board of health*

164. *No tickey no laundry*

165. *It's a dirty job but somebody got to do it*

166. *Romance without finance don't stand a chance*

167. *Who's your daddy, who you gonna love*

168. *Stupid is as stupid does*

169. *God takes care of babies, drunks and fools*

170. *Hush that fuss*

171.  *Much a blige*

172.  *Right-yonder*

173.  *Your eyes may shine, your teeth may grit but none of this will you git*

174.  *It's nothing like getting what you think you want*

175.  *That don't amount to a hill of beans.*

176.  *When you see the saw dust flying you know the mill ain't far*

177.  *Why buy the cow when you can get the milk for free*

178.  *Every man got to ride his own mighty cloud of joy*

179.  *You don't miss your water until the well runs dry*

180.  *Get your ducks in a row*

181. Get your house in order

182. Momma's baby and daddy's maybe

183. Got to many cooks in the kitchen

184. Don't take no wooden nickels

185. They are just like crabs in a barrel

186. It ain't no fun when the rabbit got the gun

187. God works in mysterious ways

188. A dog that will bring a bone will sho-nuff carry a bone

189. Let it roll off your back like a duck in the rain

190. He can sell ice to Eskimos

191. *Cheaters never win*

192. *Don't nobody want a bone but a dog*

193. *They think Mr. Charlie's ice is colder*

194. *The Lord will make a way some how*

195. *Money is the root of all evil*

196. *Six in one hand half a dozen in the other*

197. *One mans trash is another mans treasure*

198. *A closed mouth doesn't get fed*

199. *Time flies when you're having fun*

200. *Fool me once shame on you fool me twice shame on me*

201. If it looks like a duck and walks like a duck it must be a duck

202. You can put lipstick on a pig but its still a pig

203. Its my way or the highway

204. Still waters run deep

205. You play with fire you get burnt

206. Where there's smoke there's fire

207. You make your bed you got to lie in it

208. I pay the cost to be the boss

209. He who pays the piper names the tune

210. Don't make a mountain out of a molehill

211. *Its raining cats and dogs*

212. *You gotta know when to hold em and when to fold em*

213. *If the shoe fits wear it*

214. *Piss in my eye and tell me it's rain*

215. *Its a thin line between love and hated*

216. *Birds of a feather flock together*

217. *Let sleeping dogs lie*

218. *Don't throw the baby out with the bath water*

219. *It's your thing do what you wanna do*

220. *Jesus on the Mainline tell Him what you want*

221. *She lies like a rug*

222. *Age ain't nuthin but a number*

223. *If it ain't broke don't fix it*

224. *It takes two to tango*

225. *Don't throw the rock then hide your hand*

226. *So glad I woke up clothed in my right mind*

227. *Sometimes you gotta get your hands dirty*

228. *You win some you lose some*

229. *Its not about winning its how you play the game*

230. *Time waits for no man*

231. *Trying to make a dollar out of 15 cents*

232. *A tiger never changes its strips*

233. *Beating a dead horse*

234. *Its cheaper to keep her*

235. *No love lost between them*

236. *All I want is a piece of the pie*

237. *What happens in this house stays in this house*

238. *Don't spill the beans*

239. *Don't cry over spilled milk*

240. *Blind as a bat*

241. *No news is good news*

242. *If you don't have nothing nice to say don't say nothing at all*

243. *Jesus take the wheel*

244. *Back to the drawing board*

245. *Don't put your foot in your mouth*

246. *He beat her like he was beating a rattle snake*

247. *This is where the rubber meets the road*

248. *Where there's smoke there's fire*

249. *Sh\*t or get off the pot*

250. *As long as I owe you you'll never be broke*

251. The apple don't fall far from the tree

252. He's a little piss ant

253. Red red pee in the bed lick it up with jelly and bread

254. Don't be stuck on stupid

255. The mind is a terrible thing to waste

256. If you like it I love it

257. You got to bring some ass to beat some ass

258. Mind your business

259. Sugar Honey Ice Tea

260. Kiss my grits

261. *Your head is so pointy you think you are sharp*

262. *You all in the Kool-aid and don't know the flavor*

263. *Iron and steel will wear out so will flesh and bones*

264. *Don't hang with zeros*

265. *Bigger birds on higher limbs*

266. *A woman is like a bus you miss one another is coming in 15 minutes*

267. *Farrows know all medlows*

268. *Keep picking cotton and making plans*

269. *You too good til' you no good*

270. *Sometimes you got to cuss them out until they remember next time.*

271. *If it ain't one thing it's another*

272. *If It ain't one thing it's two or three*

273. *You don't use your head for anything but hat rack*

274. *I can look through water and see dry land*

275. *Mean what you say and say what you mean*

276. *Still waters run deep*

277. *Your attitude is going to get you some assitude*

278. *At first you don't succeed try try again*

279. *Nothing beats a failure but a try*

280. *You gonna catch the death of pneumonia*

281.   *You need a hot toddy*

282.   *If you don't know what to do with a little, you won't know what to do with a lot*

283.   *Bless your heart*

284.   *Shut yo mouth*

285.   *They eat and sh\*t like we do*

286.   *It's twicks here and there*

287.   *From huh to yunda*

288.   *Empty the beer bottle*

289.   *(HBO) Help a brother out*

290.   *Sometimes you got to toot your own horn*

291.  *Chew the meat and spit out the bones*

292.  *You are so bright they should call you sunny*

293.  *All is fair in love and war*

294.  *Stay out of grown folks business*

295.  *Put that in your pipe and smoke it*

296.  *You can't have your cake and eat it too*

297.  *Wrong as two left feet*

298.  *Everything that shines ain't gold*

299.  *He was butt naked*

300.  *Howling at the moon*

301. Too many fish in the sea

302. Pee you/ P U

303. Don't hate the player hate the game

304. Good things come to those who wait

305. Don't judge me if you haven't walked a mile in my shoes

306. Believe half of what you see and none of what you hear

307. You break it you bought it

308. You have to know where you came from in order to know where you're going

309. A whistling woman and a crowing hen never comes to a very good end

310. Ain't that the berries

311.  As easy as sliding off a greasy log backward

312.  Barking up the wrong tree

313.  Be like the old lady who fell out of the wagon

314.  Busy as a stump-tailed cow in fly time

315.  Caught with your pants down

316.  Chugged full

317.  Do go on

318.  Don't bite off more than you can chew

319.  Don't count your chickens before they hatch

320.  Don't let the tail wag the dog

321.   Don't let your mouth overload your tail

322.   Either fish or cut bait

323.   Even a blind hog finds an acorn now and then

324.   Every dog should have a few feas

325.   Fly off the handle

326.   He got the short end of the stick

327.   Give down the country

328.   Go hog wild

329.   Go off half-cocked

330.   Go to bed with the chickens

331. Go whole hog

332. Gone back on your raisin

333. Got your feathers ruffled

334. Child, she ghetto fabulous

335. Have no axe to grind

336. Holler like a stuck pig

337. I do declare

338. In high cotton

339. In a coon's age

340. Like a bump on a log

341.  Mend fences

342.  Scarce as hen's teeth

343.  Sight for sore eyes

344.  My old stomping grounds

345.  Sun don't shine on the same dog's tail all the time

346.  That takes the cake

347.  Two shakes of a sheep's tail

348.  Well, shut my mouth

349.  Slow as molasses running uphill in the winter

350.  Hold your horses

351.    *Be back directly*

352.    *Wait a cotton pickin' minute*

353.    *Sit a spell*

354.    *Take your own sweet time*

355.    *Once in a blue moon*

356.    *In a month of Sundays*

357.    *Goin' to town*

358.    *Goin' to hell in a hand basket*

359.    *Precious*

360.    *Yes M'am/Sir*

361.   *Sug or Sugah*

362.   *Cute as a button*

363.   *Mind your P's & Q's*

364.   *How's yer mama' n them*

365.   *Say yer prayers/the blessin'*

366.   *Oh suga foot*

367.   *Suga britches*

368.   *Heavens to Betsy*

369.   *Suppa time*

370.   *What in the Sam hill*

371. *I suwanne*

372. *What in tarnation*

373. *Well, I'll be*

374. *Up and at'em*

375. *Y'all*

376. *All Y'all*

377. *Buggy*

378. *Gizzard*

379. *Clodhopper*

380. *Whatever suits your fancy*

381. Happier than a dead pig in the sunshine

382. Wound tighter than a clock

383. Like white on rice

384. Proud as a peacock

385. Sick as a dawg

386. Don't hold water

387. Just like a bad refrigerator (Ice Box)

388. Knee high to a bullfrog/ grasshopper/ duck

389. Hotter than hell

390. The bigger they are the harder they fall

391.  *Playin' possum*

392.  *Deader than a door nail*

393.  *Plumb tuckered out*

394.  *Tickled pink*

395.  *Madder than a wet hen*

396.  *Gettin' on my last nerve*

397.  *Slap you silly*

398.  *Me Myself and I*

399.  *Fit to be tied*

400.  *Don't get your feathers ruffled*

401. *The Lord will make a way somehow*

402. *Go outside and get me a switch*

403. *Gonna get a lickin'*

404. *Hush up*

405. *Fine and Dandy*

406. *Pinch a plug out of you*

407. *Quit yer bellyachin'*

408. *Quit bein' ugly*

409. *Flew off the handle*

410. *Cut that out*

411. Raisin' cane

412. Like a bull in a china shop

413. Stinks to high heavens

414. You ain't right

415. Ragamuffin

416. High as a kite

417. Your face is gonna freeze like that

418. You weren't raised in a barn

419. Little Miss Prissy

420. Not the sharpest tool in the shed

421.   It's colder than a mother-in-law's love

422.   Ding-dong

423.   Lyin' like a dawg on a rug

424.   Ain't just whistlin' Dixie

425.   Slap yer mama

426.   Sweatin' like a sinner in church

427.   Hug yer neck

428.   Gimme some sugar

429.   Barkin' up the wrong tree

430.   You can be in the slum but the slum don't have to be in you

431.  *Your ears musta been burnin*

432.  *Goodness gracious*

433.  *Well I declare*

434.  *You can't make a silk purse out of a sow's ear*

435.  *Beatin' around the bush*

436.  *Fine as frog's hair split four ways*

437.  *Aggravating as a rock*

438.  *She would argue with a fence post*

439.  *Your mouth can block your blessings*

440.  *Trouble don't last always*

441.  He's got a burr in his saddle

442.  His knickers are in a knot

443.  He can step in sh*t and come out smelling like a rose

444.  She has a hissy fit with a tail on it

445.  He has a duck fit

446.  She has a dying duck fit

447.  You're lower than a snake's belly in a wagon rut

448.  He's slicker'n owl sh*t

449.  She's meaner than a wet panther

450.  He's a snake in the grass

451. *Why, that egg-suckin' dawg*

452. *I been running all over hell's half acre*

453. *She's busier than a cat covering crap on a marble floor*

454. *I'm as busy as a one-legged cat in a sandbox*

455. *Busier than a moth in a mitten*

456. *She is about two sandwiches shy of a picnic*

457. *She ain't nothing but a gold digger*

458. *She's stuck up higher than a light-pole*

459. *She has her nose so high in the air she could drown in a rainstorm*

460. *He thinks the sun comes up just to hear him crow*

461. He squeezes a quarter so tight the eagle screams

462. He's tighter than a bull's ass at fly time

463. Tighter than a flea's ass over a rain barrel

464. He's so cheap he wouldn't give a nickel to see Jesus ridin' a bicycle

465. Too poor to paint, too proud to whitewash

466. I'm as poor as a church mouse

467. I'm so poor I can't afford to pay attention

468. He was so poor, he had a tumbleweed as a pet

469. I couldn't buy a hummingbird on a string for a nickel

470. I'm so poor I couldn't jump over a nickel to save a dime

471. *She is sharper than Mattie was when Dick died*

472. *Those pants were so tight I could see her religion*

473. *You're gonna have old and new-monia dressed like that*

474. *Lawd, people will be able to see Christmas*

475. *Lawd, pull that down We kin see clear to the promised land*

476. *It's so dry the trees are bribing the dogs*

477. *I swan, you all musta pissed God off somehow. It's drier than popcorn fart'round these parts*

478. *He doesn't know whether to check his ass or scratch his watch*

479. *He couldn't find his ass with both hands in his back pockets*

480. *He's about as confused as a fart in a fan factory*

481.  She's lost as last year's Easter egg

482.  These people don't know which way is up

483.  He's as happy as if he had good sense.

484.  Happier than ol' Blue layin' on the porch chewin' on a big ol' catfish head

485.  You ain't nothing but a Jive Turkey

486.  Grinnin' like a possum eatin' a sweet tater

487.  Well that just dills my pickle

488.  Won't hit a lick at a snake

489.  He's about as useful as a steering wheel on a mule

490.  Over-the-shoulder boulder holders

491. *She gets my goose*

492. *He just makes my ass itch*

493. *Yankees are like hemorrhoids: Pain in the butt when they come down and always a relief when they go back up*

494. *That would make a bishop mad enough to kick in stained glass windows*

495. *She could make a preacher cuss*

496. *She could piss off the pope*

497. *If you don't stop that crying, I'll give you something to cry about*

498. *She could start an argument in an empty house*

499. *He is sharp as a tack*

500. *That makes about as much sense as tits on a bull*

501. *Quit goin' around your ass to get to your elbow.*

502. *Don't piss on my leg and tell me it's rainin'*

503. *Don't pee down my back and tell me it's raining*

504. *That dog won't hunt*

505. *You're lyin' like a no-legged dog*

506. *If his lips's movin', he's lyin'*

507. *You'd call an alligator a lizard*

508. *That man is talking with his tongue out of his shoe*

509. *He's as windy as a sack full of farts*

510. *Lying like a rug*

511. If that boy had an idea, it would die of loneliness.

512. The porch light's on, but no one's home.

513. He's only got one oar in the water.

514. If brains were leather, he wouldn't have enough to saddle a junebug

515. He's so dumb, he could throw himself on the ground and miss

516. He hasn't got the sense God gave a goose

517. When the Lord was handin' out brains, that fool thought God said trains, and he passed 'cause he don't like to travel

518. His brain rattles around like a BB in a boxcar

519. There's a tree stump in a Louisiana swamp with a higher IQ

520. You got to have a "J-O-B" if you want to be with me

521. He don't know sh*t from shinola

522. If his brains were dynamite, he couldn't blow his nose

523. Because there's snow on the roof doesn't mean that there's no fire in the furnace

524. Well butter my butt and call me a biscuit

525. Well, slap my head and call me silly

526. You little cotton-picker

527. He smelled bad enough to gag a maggot

528. Something smells bad enough to knock a dog off a gut wagon

529. I'm gonna cut your tail

530. I'm gonna jerk her bald

531. *Keep it up and I'll cancel your birth certificate*

532. *I am going to jerk a knot in your tail*

533. *You don't know dip sh\*\* from apple butter*

534. *Me-n-you are gonna mix*

535. *You don't watch out, I'm gonna cream yo' corn*

536. *You better give your heart to Jesus,'cause your butt is mine*

537. *I'll slap you to sleep, then slap you for sleeping*

538. *I'm gonna tan your hide*

539. *I'll knock you into the middle of next week looking both ways for Sunday*

540. *I'll knock you so hard you'll see tomorrow today*

541. *She's my sunshine on a cloudy day*

542. *Faster than a one-legged man in a buttkicking competition.*

543. *Faster than green grass through a goose*

544. *Faster than a hot knife through butter*

545. *Slower than a Sunday afternoon*

546. *April showers bring May flowers*

547. *We're off like a herd of turtles*

548. *He ran like a scalded haint*

549. *It happened faster than a knife fight in a phone booth*

550. *He's so ugly, he didn't get hit with the ugly stick, he got whopped with the whole forest*

551. *He fell out of the ugly tree and hit every branch on the way down*

552. *She so ugly she'd make a freight train take a dirt road*

553. *He so ugly he'd scare a buzzard off a gut pile*

554. *She's so ugly I'd hire her to haunt a house*

555. *If I had a dog as ugly as you, I'd shave his butt and make him walk backwards*

556. *She is so ugly, her face would turn sweet milk to clabber*

557. *I feel like I've been chewed up and spit out*

558. *I feel like I been'et by a wolf and sh\*t over a cliff*

559. *He looks like ten miles of bad road*

560. *You look like you've been rode hard and put up wet*

561. *Fat as a tick*

562. *He's cooler than Cola on ice*

563. *He's so skinny, if he stood sideways and stuck out his tongue, he'd look like a zipper*

564. *She's so skinny, you can't even see her shadow*

565. *She's spread out like a cold supper*

566. *If he were an inch taller, he'd be round*

567. *Sh\*ttin' in high cotton*

568. *He's richer'n Croesus*

569. *He's so rich he buys a new boat when he gets the other one wet*

570. *I'm so hungry my belly thinks my throat's been cut*

571. I'm so hungry I could eat the north end of a south- bound goat

572. Colder than a well digger's butt in January

573. It was colder than a witch's tit in a brass bra

574. That rain was a real frogwash

575. It rained like a cow pissin' on a flat rock

576. Hotter than blue blazes

577. It's colder than a penguin's balls

578. It's hotter than two rabbits screwin' in a wool sock

579. It's cold enough to freeze the balls off a pool table

580. Colder than a banker's heart on foreclosure day at the widows' and orphans' home

581. It's been hotter'n a goat's butt in a pepper patch

582. It's cold enough to freeze the tit off a frog

583. It is hotter than a jalapeño's coochie

584. There's more than one way to skin a cat

585. Bless your pea-pickin' little heart

586. Kiss my go-to-hell

587. I wouldn't walk across the street to piss on him if he was on fire

588. If you can't run with the big dogs, stay on the porch

589. Why so sad? Did Chevrolet stop makin' trucks

590. Deep in the South sushi is still called bait

591.  *He's about as useful as a screen door on a submarine*

592.  *That sticks in your throat like a hair in a biscuit*

593.  *You're so fulla sh\*t your eyes are brown*

594.  *He was as nervous as a long-tailed cat in a room full of rocking chairs*

595.  *Wrong as two left shoes*

596.  *The blacker the berry the sweeter the juice*

597.  *Talk is cheap*

598.  *Actions speak louder than words*

599.  *Beauty is only skin deep and ugly is too the bone*

600.  *You get what you give*

601. *Nuthin' comes to a sleeper but a dream*

602. *You can't teach an old dog new tricks*

603. *Papa was a rolling stone wherever he laid his hat was his home*

604. *Put ya money where your mouth is*

605. *Girl you, preaching to the choir*

606. *I heard it through the grapevine*

607. *Keepin up with the Jones'*

608. *He's just like a rabbit jumping from hole to hole*

609. *If you lie...you steal...if you steal...you kill*

610. *Dont let your mouth write a check your ass can't cash*

611.   He's crying wolf

612.   Ain't nuthin' going on but the rent

613.   Speak when spoken to

614.   That suga daddy gonna rot her teeth

615.   Monkey see monkey do, monkey look just like you

616.   When you in Rome you do as the Romans do

617.   I'll slap the taste out ya mouth

618.   You gotta beat them to the punch

619.   She wears her feelings on her sleeves

620.   Tell the truth and shame the devil

621. *You gotta climb the ladder to get to the roof*

622. *What goes around comes around*

623. *Talkin' loud and sayin' nuthin'*

624. *You may start it but imma' finish it*

625. *Keep your friends close and your enemies closer*

626. *If you live in a glass house you shouldn't throw stones*

627. *You can run but you can't hide*

628. *Pretty is as pretty does*

629. *Eat your food and let that shut your mouth*

630. *Don't use your fingers use your bread as your pusher*

631.   *You ain't seen nothing yet*

632.   *If a bullfrog had wings he wouldn't bump his ass when he jumped*

633.   *Close that hole*

634.   *Your ass is grass and I'm the lawnmower*

635.   *Don't you make eyes at me boy*

636.   *Opinions are like assholes some are just louder and smellier than others*

637.   *Flatter than a gander's arch*

638.   *That woman had forty'leven kids*

639.   *I had to go around my elbow to get to my thumb'*

640.   *He's so clumsy he'd trip over a cordless phone*

641. He's about as handy as a back pocket on a shirt

642. Shake what your momma gave ya

643. He couldn't carry a tune if he had a bucket with a lid on it

644. She was so tall she could hunt geese with a rake

645. She was so tall if she fell down she would be halfway home

646. He was so fat it was easier to go over top of him than around him

647. Poppa don't take no mess

648. No I'm not falling asleep I was just checking for holes in my eyelids

649. Bill's busier than a one-legged man at a butt kickin contest

650. Faster than a bell clapper in a goose's ass

651.   Gad night a livin'

652.   Higher than a Georgia pine

653.   I'm fixin' to go down the road a piece

654.   Well, I'll just swaney

655.   Don't go off with your pistol half cocked

656.   We better git on the stick

657.   Dumb as a bucket of rocks

658.   She's got more nerve than Carter's got Liver Pills

659.   He older than dirt

660.   She's the knee-baby of the family

661. *I feel like the last pea at pea-time*

662. *He wouldn't pay a dime to see a pissant pull a freight train*

663. *He'd have to stand up twice to cast a shadow*

664. *She'd complain if Jesus Christ came down and handed her a $5 bill*

665. *It's drier than happy hour at the Betty Ford clinic*

666. *I'm happier than a dog with two peters*

667. *I'll knock you in the head and tell God you died*

668. *She always looks like she stepped out of a band box*

669. *Act like you got some raising*

670. *You're the spitting image of your mother/ father*

671. *Sunday go-to-meetin' clothes*

672. *Fish or cut bait*

673. *Egg-sucking dawg*

674. *I'm goin to the Juke joints*

675. *Drunker than Cooter Brown*

676. *Well he/she's just down rite sorry*

677. *Plumb fell off*

678. *You sure are poor*

679. *Well if that don't put pepper in the gumbo*

680. *He could tear up a railroad track with a rubber hammer*

681.  *You must of spit that baby out*

682.  *Well thank you Billy Sunday*

683.  *If wishes were horses, then beggars would ride*

684.  *Go cut me a switch*

685.  *You better straighten up and fly right*

686.  *I'll knock your teeth down your throat and you'll spit'em out in single file*

687.  *Knee high to a grasshopper*

688.  *It's colder than Digger O'Dell, the friendly undertaker*

689.  *Well ain't he just the tom-cat's kitten*

690.  *I swalla'd down my Sun'de throat*

691. *Wash down as far as Possible, wash up as far as Possible, then wash Possible*

692. *I swanky Mama shoulda named me Grace*

693. *Well he's got the same britches to get glad in*

694. *Get your butt off your shoulders*

695. *It's no skin off my nose if he wants to do that*

696. *God love 'im somebody's gotta*

697. *Too many chiefs and not enough Indians*

698. *If you lost something look where it ain't*

699. *What you do in the dark will come to the light*

700. *I'm on my way to see a dog about pig*

701.   A little bird told me

702.   What's good for the goose is good for the gander

703.   When I get on you I am going to pay you for old and new

704.   Blessed are the brief

705.   A hit dog will holla

706.   She ain't nothing but an old nasty hoe

707.   He's my sugar-daddy

708.   He's got a big old Tombstone on top of a little dead body

709.   You can't judge a book by its cover

710.   The more you cry the less you piss

711. *A penny saved is a penny earned*

712. *A rolling stone gathers no moss*

713. *All that glitters is not gold*

714. *An empty wagon makes a lot of noise*

715. *Tip for the day Look both ways before crossing the streets*

716. *A stitch in time saves nine*

717. *A wise man listens to his own conscience*

718. *Back seat driver*

719. *Be careful what you wish for you might get it*

720. *Be that as it may*

721.   Better safe than sorry

722.   Beware of burning your bridges when you cross them

723.   Black sheep of the family

724.   Blind in one eye and can't see out of the other

725.   Blood is thicker than water

726.   Break a mirror and you will have seven years bad luck

727.   Burning the candle at both ends

728.   Burning the midnight oil

729.   Calm before the storm

730.   Can't live with them and can't live without them

731. Can't see the forest for the trees

732. Catch some Z's

733. Caught between a rock and a hard place

734. Clothes don't make the man

735. Cloud nine

736. Coast is clear

737. Cold as ice

738. Cold hands- warm heart

739. Cold shoulder

740. Cold turkey

741.  Come hell or high water

742.  Cooked his goose

743.  Ya'll gonna make me loose my mind and hurt somebody

744.  Couldn't hit the broad side of the barn

745.  Count your blessings, not your problems

746.  Day late and a dollar short

747.  Dead as a doornail

748.  Dead men tells no tales

749.  Dig your own grave

750.  Do as I say do and not as I do

751. *Do or die*

752. *Doesn't have a leg to stand on*

753. *Doesn't have two nickels to rub together*

754. *Don't bite off more that you can chew*

755. *Don't bite the hand that feeds you*

756. *You bout to speak out*

757. *Don't beat a dead dog*

758. *Your eyes are bigger than your stomach*

759. *Don't beat around the bush*

760. *Double dog dare*

761.  Easy come easy go

762.  Eat crow

763.  Eat drink and be merry

764.  Eat your heart out

765.  Eaten out of house and home

766.  Enough is enough

767.  Experience is the best teacher

768.  Fair weather friend

769.  Few and far between

770.  Fit to be tied

771.  Fits him to a T

772.  Go for broke

773.  Go off half cocked

774.  Go with the flow

775.  God helps those who help themselves

776.  God moves in mysterious ways

777.  God bless the child who has his own

778.  Going to be a cold day in hell

779.  Goodie two shoes

780.  Got my mojo working

781.  I can't make head or tails of it

782.  If you are not part of the solution, you are part of the problem

783.  If you can't beat them join them

784.  Shake rattle and roll

785.  Time to cut a rug

786.  If you can't say anything nice don't say anything

787.  If you can't stand the heat, get out of the kitchen

788.  Just hunkey dory

789.  Knock on wood

790.  Lesser of two evils

791. *It ain't over til the fat lady sings*

792. *God don't like ugly*

793. *That's funny as a three-legged dog in a horse race*

794. *Give him two nickels for a dime and he'll think he's rich*

795. *I'm busier than a 2-dollar whore on nickel night*

796. *She can start an argument in an empty house*

797. *The porch light is on but no one is home*

798. *Running like a chicken with it's head cut off*

799. *He's one fry short of a Happy Meal*

800. *If everything is coming your way you're in the wrong lane*

801.  I know better than to be all up in my head all by myself

802.  Twos and fews

803.  Keep that same energy

804.  If you see me talking to myself, it's ok. I'm having a staff meeting.

805.  Put some respect on my name

806.  Walking around with a mouth full of scripture and a heart full of hate

807.  A word to the wise should be sufficient

808.  That jewelry hanging out of your nose is about as attractive as a booger.

809.  Got more Butt than an ashtray

810.  Make sure you got clean underwear with no holes in them in case you get sick or in an accident

811.   People get mad at funerals because their names aren't on or in the program. Just be grateful your name isn't on the cover!

812.   What happens in Vegas stays in Vegas.

813.   A delay is not a denial

814.   Stop Penny Pinching

815.   Yesterday's glamour and today's charm will not pay tomorrow's rent

816.   She is just a Plain Jane

817.   If he brings you to it, he'll bring you through it

818.   Just because you dress up for Halloween does not mean you worship the devil.

819.   Just because you dress up for church does not mean you worship God.

820.   Don't fall for the okey-doke

821. *Use your head for more than a hat rack*

822. *If a man's feet stank, his àss ain't far behind*

823. *Ain't God good*

824. *Don't take my kindness for weakness.*

825. *What's good for the goose is good for the gander.*

826. *All's fair is love and war.*

827. *A hard head makes a soft behind.*

828. *We will cross that road when we get to it.*

829. *Charge it to my head and not my heart.*

830. *Eating humble pie*

831. *You have to look deep to find the deep things,*

832. *If all you do in life is stay at the surface, you will never find the things worth exploring.*

833. *You have to know when to hold them when to fold them when to walk away, and when to run.*

834. *If you're faithful over a few things, God will make you ruler over many.*

835. *You only get out of life what you put in.*

836. *Work hard, play hard.*

837. *Don't put off tomorrow what you could do today.*

838. *Tomorrow is not promised.*

839. *Time waits for no one.*

840. *Keep your head out of the clouds.*

841. I get mean when you mess with my green.

842. Speak when spoken to.

843. She takes no tea for the fever.

844. Too blessed to be stressed

845. I stay ready so that I don't have to get ready.

846. Don't jump the gun.

847. Keep your head on a swivel.

848. Watch your mouth because it may get you into something you're behind can't get you out of.

849. Two wrongs don't make a right.

850. Turn that frown upside down.

851.  Hurt people hurt people.

852.  Keep your friends close and your enemies closer.

853.  Guard your heart with all diligence

854.  Don't throw in the towel; stay at the fight.

855.  If you don't succeed at first, shake yourself off and try again.

856.  You think you're slick, but slick ain't nothing to a can of oil.

857.  When the going gets tough, the tough gets going.

858.  Old as arithmetic

859.  Every woman should have a BMW (black man working)

860.  He who angers you - controls you

861. *A new level, a new devil*

862. *I need a particular dose of the Holy Ghost*

863. *Get better or get bitter*

864. *You never know how precious your mother's voice is until you can no longer hear it.*

865. *When you throw someone under the bus. Please know the back tires will eventually run you over.*

866. *Snitches Get Stitches*

867. *I don't care how hard the pastor pushes my forehead; I'm not falling out.*

868. *Disrespect will close doors that apologies can't reopen.*

869. *Don't let the cat out of the bag*

870. *You better tighten-up before I lighten up your ass*

871. *A man who chases two rabbits catches neither*

872. *If my mouth doesn't say it, my face certainly will*

873. *You better be home when the street lights come on*

874. *Watching Church on a live stream is like watching a fireplace on a screen—you see it but don't feel the warmth!*

875. *Turn a Blind Eye*

876. *Sometimes you have to water your own plants*

877. *Broken crayons still color*

878. *Caught with your hand in the cookie jar*

879. *A raisin could be in the sun, but it cannot be in the potato salad*

880. *You sure are dripping today*

881. *The drip is in the details*

882. *You hear me, what I say*

883. *God knows my heart*

884. *If I would've could've should've*

885. *If you are not teachable, you can't grow*

886. *Who does that*

887. *Go for the Gold*

888. *Go for broke*

889. *Your opinion of others will most likely be their opinion of you*

890. *Outin the lights*

891. *Show your true colors*

892. *Sell you down the river*

893. *One for the road*

894. *Throw the cow over the fence instead of some hay*

895. *If it's important to you, you will find a way. If it's not, you will find an excuse.*

896. *Go piss up a rope*

897. *I'm serious as a heart attack*

898. *You're a liar from the grave to the pit of hell*

899. *I'm gonna turn your tucker box inside out*

900. *The early bird gets the worm, but the second mouse gets the cheese.*

901.  *What happens in Vegas stays in Vegas.*

902.  *You are not making a mess, then you are not cooking.*

903.  *Sop it up*

904.  *A positive mind and a pure heart will take you a long way.*

905.  *What's that got to do with the price of tea in China?*

906.  *I don't chew my cabbage twice.*

907.  *You are like two left shoes you can't get right*

908.  *You can roll them, but I can Swole them.*

909.  *What can I do you for?*

910.  *Act your age, not your shoe size*

911.  *They are Piss Poor*

912.  *This is gonna hurt me more than hurt you*

913.  *You can fool some of the people some of the time but you can't fool mom*

914.  *Well, life goes on*

915.  *When you do right by people...God will do right by you.*

916.  *Don't let other people put their trash in your trashcan.*

917.  *Oh dear Gussie*

918.  *Don't be the frog in the pot and let the water boil up*

919.  *Ain't nobody got time for that*

920.  *All right there now*

921. *Homie, don't play that*

922. *You gonna learn today*

923. *Go to heaven*

924. *The gift that keeps on giving*

925. *Good golly, Miss Molly*

926. *Can't have a good day with a bad attitude*

927. *Can't have a bad day with a good attitude*

928. *Where's the beef*

929. *When it rains, it pours*

930. *Dreams do come true*

931.  *Wakanda Forever*

932.  *Give it up, turn it loose*

933.  *Many hands make light work.*

934.  *A stitch in time saves nine.*

935.  *Absence makes the heart grow fonder.*

936.  *Never look a gift horse in the mouth.*

937.  *People who live in glass houses shouldn't throw stones.*

938.  *I'm blessed and highly favored*

939.  *Early to bed and early to rise make you healthy, wealthy, and wise*

940.  *Any job worth doing is worth doing well*

941. *Worthless as gum on a bootheel*

942. *One monkey don't stop the show*

943. *City lights got nothin' on country nights.*

944. *I would rather hear cows mooing and roosters crowing than horns honking.*

945. *Country is the way you live. Not the way you look*

946. *Cowgirls are God's wildest angels. They have cowboy hats for halos and horses for wings.*

947. *Everything has beauty, but not everyone sees it.*

948. *Forget glass slippers. This princess wears cowgirl boots.*

949. *Can't, never could.*

950. *A rising tide lifts all boats.*

951.  *Make hay while the sun shines.*

952.  *You can't make an omelet without breaking a few eggs*

953.  *Hurry up, we're burning daylight.*

954.  *This isn't my first rodeo.*

955.  *You're a day late and a dollar short.*

956.  *Too many cooks spoil the gravy.*

957.  *Don't buy a pig in a poke.*

958.  *As long as I owe you, you will never go broke*

959.  *Don't mistake endurance for hospitality.*

960.  *A thing of beauty is a joy forever.*

961.   *A trouble shared is a trouble halved.*

962.   *Share and share alike.*

963.   *You're the bee's knees.*

964.   *I love you with a bushel, a peck, and a hug around the neck.*

965.   *You're the cat's meow.*

966.   *It doesn't cut the mustard.*

967.   *There's more than one way to skin a cat.*

968.   *More than you can shake a stick at.*

969.   *It doesn't amount to a hill of beans.*

970.   *As I live and breathe.*

971.   Oh, my stars.

972.   No Diggity, No Doubt

973.   Goodness gracious.

974.   Heavens to Betsy.

975.   Well, I S'wanee.

976.   There's no accounting for taste.

977.   Close the door! You're letting out all the store-bought air

978.   Do that again, and you'll get a ring upside the head

979.   You just better get glad in the same clothes (or britches) you got mad in.

980.   Check the Farmers' Almanac and make sure the fish are in the feet

981.  It's coming up a cloud

982.  I believe it's finally fairing off.

983.  It can't be sweet tea and magnolias ALL the time.

984.  I've got a hitch in my get-along.

985.  I've got a hitch in my giddy-up.

986.  Reckon I'll mosey on down the road

987.  I'll be there directly

988.  Let's go loaferin' this morning.

989.  I wish I had some ear bobs/ear screws to match this necklace

990.  Hitch your wagon to a star, honey

991. *Fit to eat*

992. *Once a man, twice a child*

993. *Don't you sass me*

994. *This tastes pretty good even if I did make it*

995. *Lordy mercy sakes, alive*

996. *Time you enjoy wasting is not wasted time*

997. *Sometimes, when things are falling apart, they may actually be falling into place*

998. *Do you give as much energy to your dreams as you do to your fears*

999. *Be you because only you can be you*

1000. *Be so happy that when other people look at you, they become happy too.*

The Honorable Reverend Dr. William Lewis Rocky Brown III, a public servant, preacher, motivationalist, counselor, and consultant. Dr. Brown is a graduate of Cheyney University, Eastern Baptist Theological Seminary, and Jameson Christian College. He has received training in nonviolent direct action from the Martin Luther King Jr. Center for Social Change in Atlanta, Georgia, and is a graduate of the University ol the Virgin Islands Institute for the Treatment of Alcoholism and Drug Addiction and the FBI and DEA Citizens Academies, Philadelphia Divisions. Dr. Brown is president and CEO of Brown and Associates, LTD. which provides anger management. DUI and drug and alcohol treatment. Dr. Brown is an ordained

Baptist minister and is presently the pastor of Youth and Community of the Bethany Baptist Church in Chester. Pennsylvania, and a master police chaplain. Dr. Brown has a weekly religious telephonic service, Saturday Night Live: Prayer and Praise, a weekly column that appears in Scoop USA and a daily blog on his website, www.yourspiritualmotivation.com. In the 80s and '90s, he traveled around the country using 'educational rap music to motivate young people to stay in school and to say no to drugs and violence. Thus, he was affectionately known as the "Rappin Rev." Dr. Brown has been actively involved in numerous community' organizations over the years. He is an ambassador for the Philadelphia division of the FBI, a chaplain for several local police departments, past-president of the Law Enforcement Chaplains of Delaware County, PA, past-state representative for the International Conference of Police Chaplains, A PA State Constable and Executive Board of the Singing Sensations Youth Choir. He is a member of the Prince Hall Masons, the Elks and Omega Psi Phi Fraternity'. His community work has earned him over 200 awards and commendations. Personal Motto:

"Lord, treat me tomorrow the way'
I treat other people today."

www.ingramcontent.com/pod-product-compliance
Lightning Source LLC
Chambersburg PA
CBHW051221120626
46547CB00013B/1447